ICT Adventure

Year 3

Pupil Book

Acknowledgements

The publisher would like to thank the following for their valuable comments and advice when trialling and reviewing ICT Adventure:

Heather Govier, chair of the charity MAPE (Micros and Primary Education)
Harriet Martin, Cofton Primary School, Birmingham
Caroline Moxon, Roundhay St John's Church of England Primary School, Leeds
Mrs Furness, Kerr Mackie Primary School, Leeds
Anna Seddon, St Cuthbert with Matthias CE School, London
D Leeming, Melcombe Primary School, London
Beth Elston

Published by Collins
An imprint of HarperCollins*Publishers* Ltd
77–85 Fulham Palace Road
Hammersmith
London
W6 8JB

www.**Collins**Education.com
On-line support for schools and colleges

First published 2003

10 9 8 7 6 5 4 3 2 1

Text: © HarperCollins*Publishers*
Spark Island illustrations: © Spark Learning Ltd

ISBN 0 00 716012 7

Carol Elston and Sue Orrell assert the moral right to be identified as the authors of this work.

British Library Cataloguing in Publication Data
A catalogue record for this publication is available from the British Library.

We are grateful to the following for permission to reproduce photographs:
BBC Weather Centre, 45; Met Office (© Crown copyright). Reproduced under Licence Number MetO/IPR/2/2003 0011, 45; Science Photo Library, 42 (x4), 43 (x4) & 44.

Design: Ken Vail Graphic Design, Cambridge
Illustrations: Mat Wells and Michelle Dunn
Cover design: Susi Martin Taylor
Printed by: Scotprint

You might also like to visit
www.**fire**and**water**.com
The book lover's website

Contents

Welcome to

This is Sidney. He is quite shy.

There are lots of others who live in Sparklantis.

The Atlanteans live in Sparklantis and are ruled by the Atlantean King and Queen. The King and Queen have two grandchildren, Piska and Pod.

Norman is a fish, but he can't swim. He lives on the seabed.

Sparklantis

The clamps are the largest creatures in Sparklantis.

The drips are made entirely from water. They live and work in the Drip Drainpipe.

The Hair Care Crew is a group of fish with hair. They live in the Haircare Cave.

Meera the dolphin is a wise and trusted friend of the Atlanteans.

Cards on the table

Cards are used to celebrate birthdays, weddings, anniversaries and many more special occasions.

The layout of the card, the type of picture used and the style of the writing, usually tell you whom the card is designed for. You can often tell what the occasion is by the writing on the front of the card.

1

2

3

4

5

6

Questions

1 These cards have all been designed for a special occasion. Can you guess what the occasions are?

2 Can you think of any other occasions where you would send a card? What type of picture would the card have on the front? What would the writing on the front say?

3 Have you spotted any unusual greeting cards recently?

The writing inside a card also gives some clues who the card might be for. Can you match the following greetings to the cards on the previous page?

A

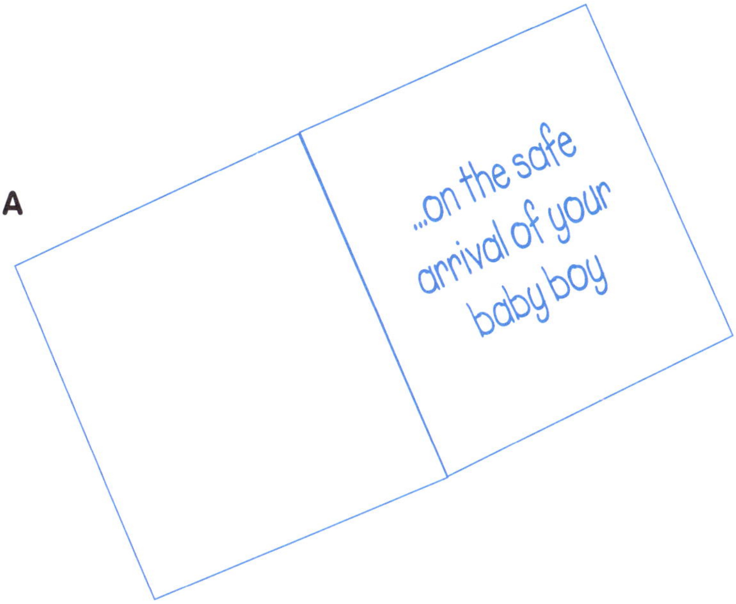

...on the safe arrival of your baby boy

B

HOPE THE SUN SHINES ON YOU AGAIN SOON

C

Many Happy Returns

D

HAVE A HAPPY HOLIDAY!

The messages inside the cards are all written using different fonts, some quite fancy and others plain. The message is large enough to be read easily and is centred on the page.

Cards on the table

By using both pictures and words, greeting cards can send a clear message. By adding pictures and changing the look of words, a document can become much more attractive. People are more likely to read it, if it catches their eye.

The Hair Care Crew is opening a new hair salon and they are holding a party to celebrate. One of the junior hairdressers has written a simple invitation, but Pauline Pike has decided to make it more eye-catching.

An invitation from the Hair Care Crew

Come to our Grand Opening Party

30th September

At the new Hair Care salon

From 6 p.m. to 8 p.m.

Plenty of food and drink provided!

See you there!

An invitation from the Hair Care Crew

Come to our Grand Opening Party
30th September

at the new Hair Care salon

from 6 p.m. to 8 p.m.
Plenty of food and drink provided!

See you there!

Questions

1 Which invitation do you prefer? Why?

2 Can you think of any examples of documents where you would not want to include pictures or fancy fonts?

Things to do at the computer

1 Finish the greeting cards: add suitable words to the picture and change the fonts.

2 Design your own birthday card.

3 Improve the appearance of an invitation to a bonfire party.

Remember

The layout and choice of words and pictures can communicate different messages.

Font fun

By changing the way that words look you can make a document much more exciting to read. Your word processor will have lots of different fonts to choose from and you can easily change the size and colour of the words, but be careful not to over do it, too many different styles and colours will make it difficult to read.

Here are just some of the fonts you may want to try.

Impact	**How does this text look?**
Tahoma	How does this text look?
Haettenschweiler	**How does this text look?**
Monotype Corsiva	*How does this text look?*
Comic Sans	How does this text look?
Palatino	How does this text look?
Arial Black	**How does this text look?**

Questions

1 Which of the fonts shown above is your favourite?

2 Why do you like it?

3 What would you use this font for?

Every picture tells a story

Word processors usually have lots of pictures that you can load into your document. You can make the pictures bigger or smaller and move them around to fit with your text. You can also search for pictures on CDs or from sites on the internet.

This document explains how to look after your teeth properly. There are also pictures to help you understand what you should do to keep your teeth and gums healthy.

Taking care of your teeth.

You need to look after your teeth. Brushing your teeth is important because it helps to stop plaque building up on them. Plaque is sticky and attracts bacteria and sugar that can damage your teeth. Follow these steps and you will have strong, healthy teeth:

Brush your teeth at least twice a day, after breakfast and again before you go to bed.

Remember to brush the sides and back of your teeth as well as the front. Brush away from your gums. Try to brush your teeth for at least two minutes!

Flossing between your teeth can help remove trapped food and plaque, it can be quite difficult to do, but keep practising!

Visit the dentist every six months to check for any damage and help make sure your teeth are really clean.

Questions

1 Do you think that the pictures help you understand how to look after your teeth?

2 Do the pictures make the document look more attractive?

Meera is teaching Pod, Piska and their friends about how plants grow on the island. Just before she starts, she drops all her notes and the words and pictures are completely muddled.

C

7 The flowers turn into fruits.

G

4 The seedling gets taller and stronger and grows its first leaves.

H

1 A seed is buried in the ground.

D

B

8 The fruit splits open and the seeds fall out.

E

A

2 A shoot comes out of the seed.

5 The seedling grows into a plant with lots of leaves.

F

6 The plant makes flowers and the bees bring pollen.

3 The seed grows into a seedling and breaks through the soil towards the light.

Question

Can you work out which picture goes with each word card?

Things to do at the computer

1 Can you find the pictures for brushing your teeth on the CD and add them to the document about taking care of your teeth? You can change their size to make them fit.

2 Can you help Meera by designing a document that she can use to give her lesson about plants?

Remember

When you have found a picture that you like, you can easily change its size to fit into your document.

 # Word play

Sometimes words can actually look like what they mean!

HUGE **BOLD**

Spidery

BANG!

Tiny

BLUE BALL BLUE BALL BLUE BALL

STAIRS

Questions

1 Can you think of any other words that could look like their meaning?

2 Can you think of an example of a document where you could use words that look like their meaning?

Pauline Pike has written this poem about living in Sparklantis.

The City of Sparklantis By Pauline Pike

Sparklantis lies beneath the waves
The home of the Atlanteans who lives in caves
They share the city with both friends and foe
Fish such as mullet, plaice, pike and rainbow
Sidney shark thinks he is the king of the sea
He is big and FIERCE but likes veggies for tea.

The Atlanteans are ruled by a Queen and a King
Who believe their children should play music and sing
But Piska and Pod like to have fun and play
They have lots of adventures every day
They are LOUD and sHOUT a lot, it's part of their charm
As the sound fades away all is calm.

The Hair Care Crew are fish with hair!
A sight so strange the other fish stare
The clamps are large it's true to say
They snap their jaws shut to catch their prey
Their prey are trapped, shivering and scared
Until they answer a riddle or do as dared.

Questions

1 Do you think the first and second verses of the poem look more interesting than the third verse? Why is this?

2 If you were going to improve the look of the third verse, which words would you change and how would you change them?

Word play

It is important that you catch the attention of your audience. You need to make sure that everyone reads the important information you have written. Be careful though, if you try to be too clever, you may end up making your poster difficult to read!

FIVE STEPS TO HEALTHY TEETH

Too many sugary foods can damage your teeth

Eat fruit and vegetables and drink plenty of milk

Every morning and evening brush your teeth

Trapped food can be removed by flossing

Have a trip to the dentist twice a year

FIVE STEPS TO HEALTHY TEETH

Too many sugary foods can damage your teeth

Eat fruit and vegetables and drink plenty of milk

Every morning and evening brush your teeth

Trapped food can be removed by flossing

Have a trip to the dentist twice a year

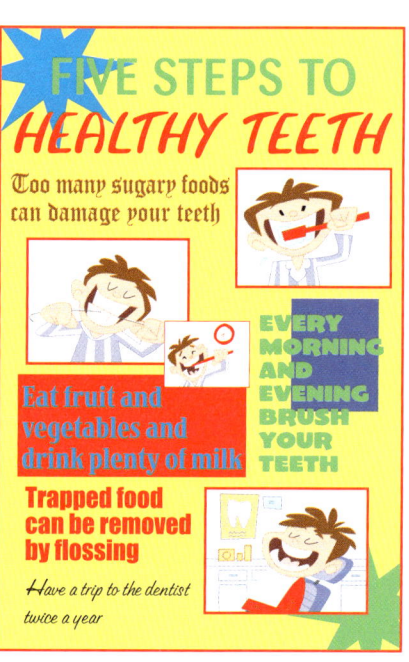

FIVE STEPS TO HEALTHY TEETH

Too many sugary foods can damage your teeth

Eat fruit and vegetables and drink plenty of milk

EVERY MORNING AND EVENING BRUSH YOUR TEETH

Trapped food can be removed by flossing

Have a trip to the dentist twice a year

Things to do at the computer

Design your own version of the Teeth poster. By changing the layout, the fonts, colours and adding pictures you can make it much more attractive!

Remember

By changing the way that words look you can make a document much more exciting to read.

Questions

1 Which poster would you stop and read?

2 Which poster is the most attractive? Why is this?

3 Which is the least attractive? Why is this?

Change it!

You can change a document by adding pictures and changing the font. You must also think about the words you use. It is important to use different words rather than repeating the same word over and over again. Look at Pod's story on the next two pages.

"I'm going to tell you a story", said Pod.
"Oh, good", said Piska, "I love your stories. Will it be scary?"
"Of course", said Pod, "my stories are always scary!"

Once upon a time, long, long ago two children called Saska and Sid lived with their mum and dad in a city called Sparklantis, which stood at the bottom of the deep sea. Saska and Sid loved to have adventures and one day they decided to visit the dark place, beyond the walls of Sparklantis.

"Let's go and see what it's like", said Sid, "it can't be that scary, the fish go there all the time."
"I'm not scared", said Saska twirling her hair around her finger.
"I can't wait to see if there really are sharks there", Sid said excitedly.

Sid and Saska set off and soon reached the city walls.

"It's very, very dark out there", Saska said nervously.
"Have you got the torch?", Sid said.
"Yes, it's in my pack", Saska said, reaching into her pack. "And I also have lots of chocolate, do you want some?"
"When have I ever said no to chocolate?", Sid said.

As they were talking, a rather large, fierce looking shark swam past the other side of the city walls. "I can smell chocolate", he said to himself as he swam towards the smell, "yum, yum chocolate for tea tonight".

Just at that moment, Sid and Saska jumped over the wall to be greeted by a large open mouth full of sharp teeth.
"Quick go back", said Saska, clambering back over the wall. But Sid was frozen to the spot. He just stood there looking at the shark, the chocolate in his hand.

"That's all for now", said Pod.
"Oh no", said Piska, "you can't leave the story there I want to know what happens next."
"Later", said Pod.

Change it!

"I'm going to tell you a story", said Pod.
"Oh, good", said Piska, "I love your stories. Will it be scary?"
"Of course", laughed Pod, "my stories are always scary!"

Once upon a time, long, long ago two children called Saska and Sid lived with their mum and dad in a city called Sparklantis which stood at the bottom of the deep sea. Saska and Sid loved to have adventures and one day they decided to visit the dark place, beyond the walls of Sparklantis.

"Let's go and see what it's like", suggested Sid, "it can't be that scary, the fish go there all the time."
"I'm not scared", murmured Saska twirling her hair around her finger.
"I can't wait to see if there really are sharks there", Sid said excitedly.

Sid and Saska set off and soon reached the city walls.

"It's very, very dark out there", Saska whispered nervously.
"Have you got the torch?", Sid asked.
"Yes, it's in my pack," Saska replied, reaching into her pack. "And I also have lots of chocolate, do you want some?"
"When have I ever said no to chocolate?", Sid laughed.

As they were talking, a rather large, fierce looking shark swam past the other side of the city walls. "I can smell chocolate", he mumbled to himself as he swam towards the smell, "yum, yum chocolate for tea tonight".

Just at that moment, Sid and Saska jumped over the wall to be greeted by a large open mouth full of sharp teeth.
"Quick go back", shrieked Saska, clambering back over the wall. But Sid was frozen to the spot. He just stood there looking at the shark, the chocolate in his hand.

"That's all for now", said Pod.
"Oh no", cried Piska, "you can't leave the story there I want to know what happens next."
"Later", laughed Pod.

Questions

1 How are the two stories different?

2 Which one is the most interesting to read?

3 What words have changed?

Things to do

Make a list of all the different words used instead of *said*. Can you think of any more? If you can, add them to your list.

Here is some more of the story. Pod has forgotten what Piska told him.
He has used the word *said* too many times again.

"Are you ready, Piska?" said Pod, "I'm going to continue with the story".
"Yes I can't wait", said Piska excitedly, "what will happen to Sid?"

Sid looked into the eyes of the shark not knowing quite what to do.
"Have you got anymore of that?" said the shark, looking hungrily at
the chocolate.

Saska peeked over the wall. "I have", she said in a small croaky
voice, "here it is, please don't eat my brother".

The shark laughed loudly. "I don't eat boys", he said, "I'm a
vegetarian. But, I do love chocolate". He licked his lips slowly and
flicked his tail from side to side.

Sid suddenly found he could move again. "Here have this", he
said, offering his chocolate to the shark. It disappeared in one bite.
"That was simply the best", the shark said, rolling his eyes
upwards. "I don't suppose you have anymore?" he said swimming
towards Saska.

Just at that moment they heard a swishing sound coming towards
them. "Quick", said the shark turning towards Sid, "get behind the
wall, the shark gang are coming. I might not eat little boys, but
they do".

Sid scrambled over the wall and crouched down beside his sister.
"Keep still and don't say a word", the shark said, "I'll deal with this".

Things to do at the computer

1 Can you improve the second part of Pod's story by
changing the word *said* to a different word? Look
back to the list you made and decide which words
you would use instead. If the word you want is not
in the word bank, type it in yourself.

2 Practise some more using the 'You're the editor'
game. You can make stories more interesting by
changing *went, really* and *nice* as well as *said*!

Remember

You can easily change
your words using a word
processor so make sure
your document
sounds good as
well as looks good!

Punctuation rules, OK?

Now that you have sorted out those repetitive words like *said, nice* and *went,* the next step is to improve your punctuation. Pod has started using different words instead of *said,* but he seems to have forgotten his punctuation.

"Sebastian is that you", a voice called from the distance.

"Yes, it's me", the chocolate loving shark replied. "what are you all doing so far from home". We thought we could smell children, the voice replied. the leader of the gang came into sight. He was twice as big as sebastian and his eyes flashed as he looked around. "have you seen any children", my friend, he asked swimming up close to Sebastian.

No, no, stuttered sebastian, why would children come here? You must be mistaken.

At that moment, sid sneezed, just a little sneeze but enough for the big shark to notice.

"What was that the big shark asked", swimming towards the wall. he was only inches away from sid and saska. They crouched together, shaking with fear. just as they thought they could bare it no longer, pauline Pike swam over their heads and towards the big shark. She fluttered past his head and then she was gone. Pauline knew that it was not a good idea to stay too close to a shark's head.

"That must be what you heard said sebastian, clearly relieved. There are definitely no children around here.

Hum, you might be right, the big shark replied, come on boys let's go home. He turned to sebastian "if you see any children, you let me know" he said.

Sebastian nodded as he watched them swim away.

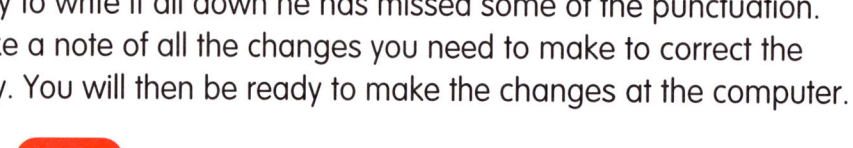

Things to do

Read the rest of Pod's story. His story is getting exciting, but in his hurry to write it all down he has missed some of the punctuation. Make a note of all the changes you need to make to correct the story. You will then be ready to make the changes at the computer.

What changes do you need to make to the punctuation in these sentences?

1 Why do I need to brush my teeth every day asked the child.

2 If you don't brush your teeth the plaque and sugar will stick to your teeth and they will start to decay, replied mr green, the dentist.

3 I really can't use this dental floss joe said crossly. it's just no use.

4 You just need to practise mr green replied. you will soon get the hang of it.

5 Look, said kate, my plants are growing. i can see their shoots coming through the soil.

6 My favourite plant is the strawberry said beth, because i love to eat the fruit.

7 can you see the new leaves coming, asked alex.

8 The bees seem to be attracted to the brightly coloured flowers the most. why is this.

Things to do at the computer

1 Look at the computer keyboard and see if you can find the answers to Pod's questions.
How do I type capital letters?
How do I type speech marks?
How do I type a question mark?
How do I type an exclamation mark?

2 Can you correct Pod's story for him?

3 Can you correct the punctuation for the sentences about teeth and plants?

Remember

By using punctuation, your writing will be much easier to read and understand.

Class booklet

Later in the year you will swap information with another school in the country. The children from the other school will want to know all about the place where you live. So, now is your chance to use all your skills to produce a booklet full of information. There will be loads of pictures, different fonts to make the words more interesting and of course, spot on punctuation!

Here are some examples of the kinds of things you may like to include in your class booklet.

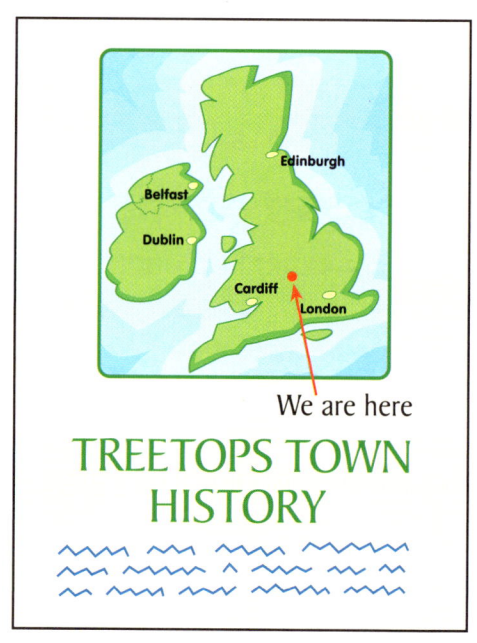

Electronic keyboard

The electronic keyboard can make the sound of lots of different instruments. Not all electronic keyboards are the same. The one you have in your school might have different keys to the one in the picture.

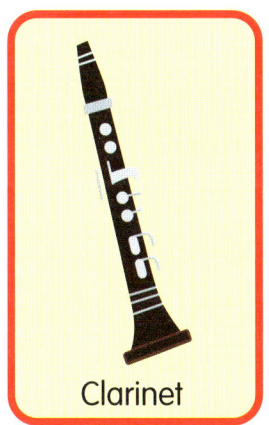

Clarinet

Guitar

Drum

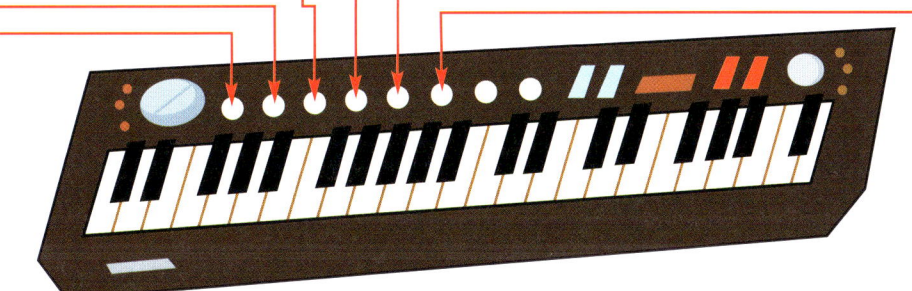

Piano

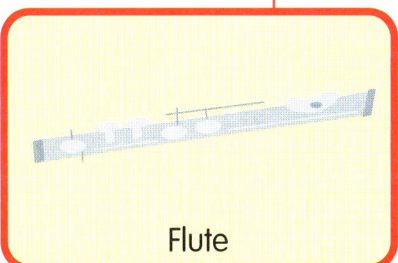

Flute

Thing to do

Listen to each sound in turn and see if you can tell which musical instrument is being played.

Questions

1 Which instrument makes your favourite sound?
2 Can you describe the sound?

Remember

An electronic keyboard can be used to select and control sounds.

ICT and music

Pod, Piska and their friends are playing in the school band.
Can you name all the instruments?

Things to do at the computer

1 Find each of the instruments in the orchestra on the CD-ROM.

2 Listen to the sound that each instrument makes.

3 Write down one interesting fact about the instrument on your musical card.

Musical instruments are grouped into families such as strings, wind, brass and percussion. You can often tell which family an instrument belongs to by the sound it makes.

Wind   **String**   **Percussion**   **Brass**

Piska is using a tape recorder to record Pod playing the drums.

Things to do

Using your musical cards, can you put the rest of the instruments played by the band into the correct families?

Can you record yourself playing an instrument?

Play it back and see if your friends can guess what instrument you are playing?

Remember

ICT can be used to make the sounds of musical instruments and it can also be used to record you playing real instruments.

Mood music

Computer programs can be used to make music. The program that Pod is using has different icons to choose from. When he clicks on an icon the program plays a short tune.

Pod has clicked on the picture of the fish. The tune reminds him of swimming in the ocean with his friends.

This is a happy memory for Pod, so the next icon he tries is the smiling face. He likes these two tunes so much, he plays them one after the other over and over again while he and Piska play along.

Things to do at the computer

1 Can you create your own melody? Listen to all of the tunes by clicking on the icons and then choose four to make up a melody. You can use the loop button to play the melody over and over again.

2 When you are happy with your melody, record it and play along, just like Pod and Piska.

Remember

You can make your own tunes using a computer program.

Class song

Meera the dolphin is going to help Pod, Piska and their friends compose a class song. She says that the best songs are simple and has suggested that they use just two of the icons to create the melody. They have decided to use the simple pattern AABA for their base melody. It was difficult for them all to agree on what two icons to use but they seem to have come to a decision!

The next step is to decide what real instruments they should play to make the song sound even better.

The tune is coming along well. Meera has divided the class into four groups and each group is going to make up some words for the song. They have written the words for one verse each. When the song is finished they will play and sing it to the rest of the school.

Things to do

Now it is your turn. Can you and your friends compose a class song? Have a go!

Remember

Use a simple pattern of musical phrases to create a great song!

Get it organised!

If you have lots of information to search through it can be difficult to find what you are looking for. To make it easier, information can be put in order.

Have a look at a telephone directory. It is full of information about the people who live in your town. It includes their name, address and telephone number. If you need to find a telephone number you can look up the name of the person.

Graves, S	7 The Broadway	(0557) 486273
Gravett, L	18 Herons Close	(0557) 357748
Gray, B	6 York Street	(0557) 374149
Gray, H	51 Crown Lane	(0557) 522671
Gray, N	5 Brookfields	(0557) 267748
Grayland, K	24 London Road	(0557) 687445
Greatbatch, N	28 The Cut	(0557) 916777
Greaves, H	54 The Paddock	(0557) 418337
Green, A	8 The Avenue	(0557) 213983
Green, D	15 Denton Street	(0557) 312564
Green, M	123 King Street	(0557) 324967
Green, S	72 New Road	(0557) 372981
Greenhill, M	111 Washington Road	(0557) 397415
Greening, C	24 The Elms	(0557) 154889
Greening, M	45 High Street	(0557) 394199
Greenway, E	29 Station Road	(0557) 648521
Greer, J	22 Spires Avenue	(0557) 369956
Gregson, T	4 Green End	(0557) 124483
Grenfell, H	19 Kings Avenue	(0557) 529975
Gresham, Y	18 Fosters Road	(0557) 399278

This telephone directory is ordered (or sorted) by the person's surname. The surnames are in alphabetical order. All the people with surnames beginning with the letter A are at the beginning of the directory and those beginning with Z are at the end. If a name starts with the letter M, you will find it somewhere near the middle of the directory.

Questions

1 Jane Morris is due to visit Mr. Green, the dentist, but she cannot remember the date of her appointment. She needs to telephone him to check the date. Can you find Mr. Green's telephone number on the page of the telephone directory?

2 There are four people with the surname Green. How can Jane find out which one is her dentist? His first name is David, does that help your search?

A telephone directory is a **database**. Each line in the telephone directory is called a **record** and each item of information in the record is called a **field**.

This is the record for Mr. Green, the dentist. The telephone directory tells us his name, initial, address and telephone number. These are the fields of the database.

Mr. Green also uses a database to help him keep track of his patients. He has a box of cards on his desk. Each card has information about a different patient.

Get it organised!

Here are some of Mr. Green's record cards.

Surname: Arnold
First name: Carl
Address: 21 Kendal Place
　　　　 Little Denton
　　　　 LD5 7BP
Telephone: (0557) 329012
Next Appointment: 3rd March, 3 p.m.

Surname: Cavner
First name: Lucy
Address: 34 Maple Lane
　　　　 Little Denton
　　　　 LD5 5QW
Telephone: (0557) 387643
Next Appointment: 23rd March, 9 a.m.

Surname: Morris
First name: Jane
Address: 56 Truman Road
　　　　 Little Denton
　　　　 LD5 6YT
Telephone: (0557) 333251
Next Appointment: 24th February, 4 p.m.

Surname: Roscoe
First name: Sami
Address: 11 Drew Bank
　　　　 Little Denton
　　　　 LD5 7TR
Telephone: (0557) 345821
Next Appointment: 21st February, 3.30 p.m.

Surname: Turner
First name: Mat
Address: 13 The Drive
　　　　 Little Denton
　　　　 LD5 8JG
Telephone: (0557) 342198
Next Appointment: 13th March, 11.30 a.m.

Surname: Zaak
First name: Cindy
Address: 26 High Street
　　　　 Little Denton
　　　　 LD5 6KJ
Telephone: (0557) 378213
Next Appointment: 17th March, 9.30 a.m.

Fields

Record

Mr. Green's box of patient cards is a database. Each card in the box is a record.

A database contains records and each record contains fields.

Questions

1 When is Jane Morris's next appointment?

2 How many records are shown?

3 How many fields are there on each record?

4 What information does the last field on each record card tell you?

5 Who lives at 11 Drew Bank?

Adding information

Mr. Green has received this letter in today's post. He needs to fill out a record card for his new patient. He can find most of the information he needs from the letter.

Surname:
First name:
Address:

Telephone:
Next Appointment:

Surname: Harman
First name: Josie
Address: 23 Grange Road
　　　　　Little Denton
　　　　　LD5 6KL
Telephone: (0557) 325711
Next Appointment: 17th February, 2 p.m.

Dear Mr. Green

My name is **Josie Harman** and I have recently moved to **Little Denton**. I am living at **23 Grange Road, LD5 6KL**. I would like to register with you and request an appointment. Could you please telephone me to let me know your first available date? My telephone number is **(0557) 325711**.

Yours sincerely,

J. Harman

Mr. Green needs to check in his appointment book. The next available appointment is on **17th February at 2 p.m**.

34 Jupiter Place
Little Denton
LD5 4RT

Dear Mr. Green,

I would like my son, Ali, to join your dental practice. Could you please arrange an appointment for him in March? I can be contacted on (0557) 349981.

Yours sincerely

Mrs. Seem

Things to do

1 Can you add Josie's details to your record cards?

2 Mr. Green has received another letter from someone who wants to join his dental practice. He has checked his appointment book and he has a space on 2nd March at 9 a.m. Can you fill in a record card for him?

Adding information

Pod, Piska and their friends are learning all about the plants that grow on Spark Island. To help them, Meera the dolphin has made a database. Each record in the database contains information on a single plant.

Name: busy lizzie
Colour: pink
First flowers in: summer
Height grows to (cm): 30
Light: sun & shade
Hardy?: no

Name: rose
Colour: red
First flowers in: summer
Height grows to (cm):100
Light: sun
Hardy?: yes

Name: pansy
Colour: purple
First flowers in: spring
Height grows to (cm): 20
Light: sun & shade
Hardy?: yes

Name: crocus
Colour: yellow
First flowers in: spring
Height grows to (cm): 7
Light: sun
Hardy?: yes

Name: foxglove
Colour: pink
First flowers in: spring
Height grows to (cm): 120
Light: sun & shade
Hardy?: yes

Name: tulip
Colour: red
First flowers in: spring
Height grows to (cm): 60
Light: sun
Hardy?: yes

Fields can contain all sorts of information, pictures, words, numbers and even answers to questions. The last field in these records contains the answer **yes** or **no**.

Questions

1 Do you know what hardy means?

2 Which field contains a number?

3 Which fields contain information as words?

4 Which field contains information as yes or no?

5 What does the picture tell us?

Things to do

Meera needs to add some more records to the database. She has written a description for each new flower. Can you find all the information needed and enter it on to blank record cards?

In the springtime, the parklands of Spark Island are full of yellow daffodils. The daffodil is a hardy plant that enjoys the sun. It raises its trumpet head towards the sky and can grow to be around 30cm tall.

The woodlands have a blue carpet in spring. The bluebell is hardy and likes to grow shaded from the sun. It grows to around 45 cm tall.

Geraniums like to be indoors. They grow best close to the windows as they like lots of sunlight. Their bright red flowers cheer up the place. They can grow outside as well but they are not hardy. In the garden, they flower in summer. They grow to about 60 cm tall.

Remember

Fields can contain pictures, words, numbers or yes or no answers.

Adding and sorting

Meera the dolphin has copied the information from all her plant record cards into a computer database. To look at each record in turn, Meera clicks on the **Next** button to move to the next record in the database and the **Back** button to move back to the record before.

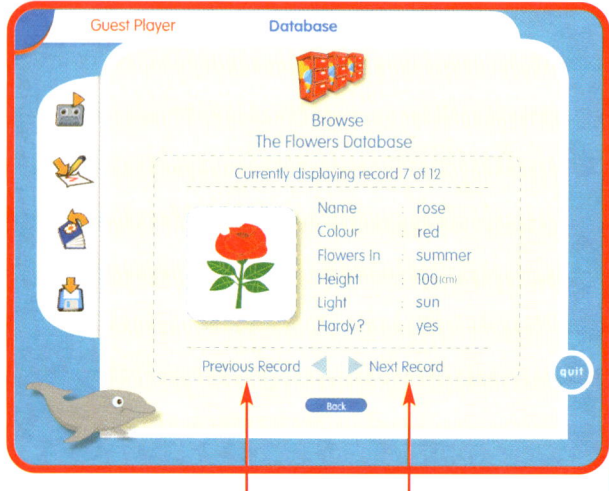

Move back a record   Move to next record

The computer records look similar to the record cards. They even have a picture of the plant.

Meera wants to add a few new records to her database. This is easy to do. First she needs to click on the **Edit** button. Then she clicks on **Add Record** and types in the information

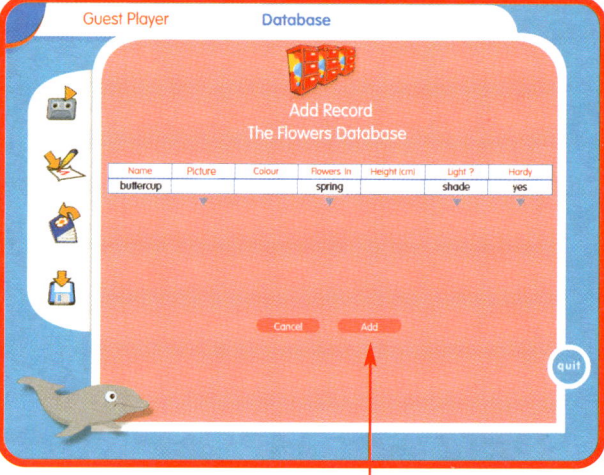

Add a new record

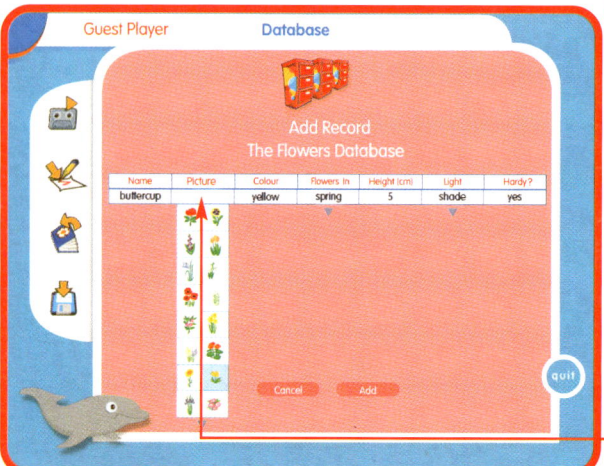

To add a picture of the flower she clicks on the arrow under the picture field. This opens a picture bank and she can choose the picture of the flower.

Add a picture

When she has entered all the information she can click on the **Add** button to add the new record to the database. She has added three new records.

Adding and sorting

If you do not have many record cards you may not need to use a computer database. With just a few records it is quite easy to find what you are looking for, but imagine if you had records for a 100 plants! Computers can work much faster than people. A computer can **sort** thousands of records into **order** in just a few seconds.

Meera wants to sort her records into alphabetical order by name. To do this, she first needs to click on the **Sort** button. She will then see a list of fields.

Sort the records —

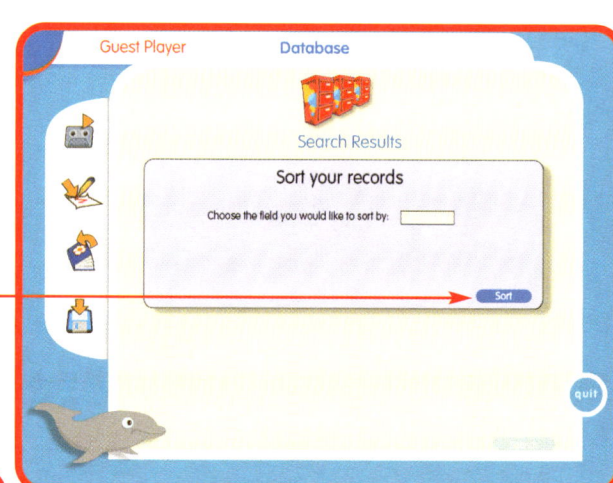

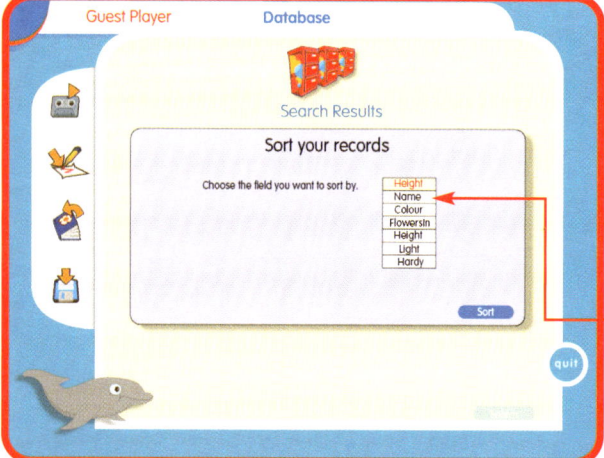

She wants to see the plants listed in alphabetical order so she clicks on the **Name** field in the drop down list.

Name field

Now that she has chosen the field to sort by, she has to press the **Sort** button again. The records are now displayed in alphabetical order. Can you spot the three new records?

Meera can display a single record by clicking on its name.

Display a single record —

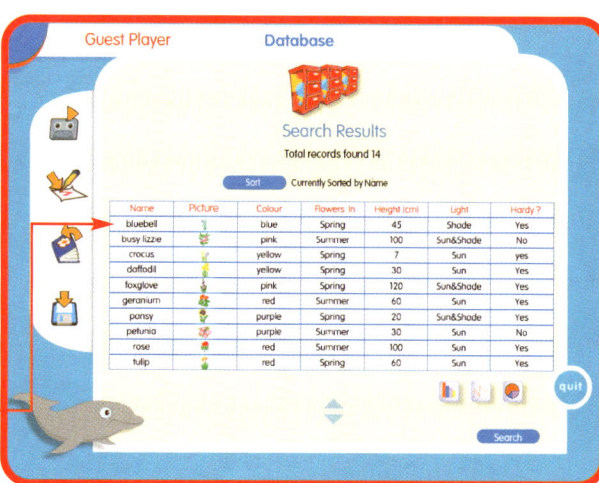

Things to do at the computer

1 Can you help Meera by adding a few more records?
Find all the information you need and enter it into the
blank record. You will also need to select the picture
of the plant from the picture bank.

The snowdrop is a hardy winter
flower. It has a bell shaped white
flower and likes sun and shade. It
grows to be 20cm tall.

The sunflower can grow to be 2 metres tall
(200cm)! It is a hardy plant that flowers in late
summer. It likes to grow in a sunny position.

The white lily is a hardy summer plant
that can grow to be 1 metre tall
(100cm). It likes plenty of sunlight.

2 Can you sort your records into alphabetical order by plant name?
Hint: Click on the **Sort** button and choose the **Name** from the list of fields.

3 Can you sort your records in order of height?

Questions

1 Did you find it easy to add the new records to
the computer database?

2 Did you find it quicker to sort the records using
the computer?

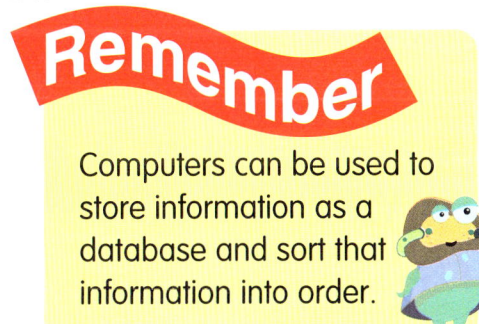

Remember

Computers can be used to
store information as a
database and sort that
information into order.

Searching

With your help, the Meera the dolphin now has 15 records in her plants database. Using the computer she can quickly search through the records to find information.

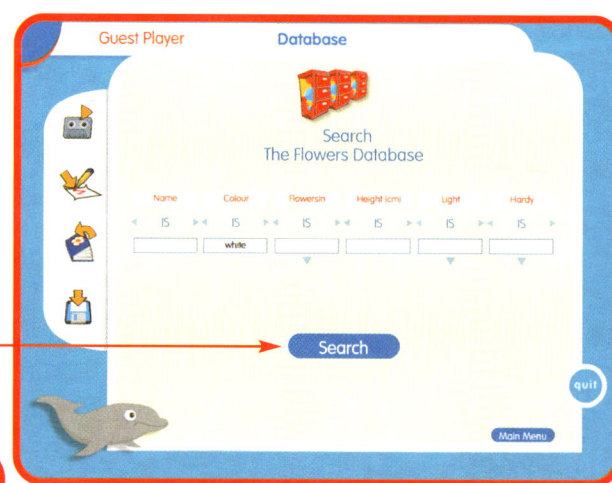

Her first search is for flowers that are white. She clicks on the **Search** button and types **white** into the **Colour** field. She then clicks **Search** again to see all the white flowers displayed in a table.

Search

When Meera clicks on the first record in the list she can see the details for the first white flower more clearly. She can click **Next** to see the next record, or **Back** to return to her search results screen.

Records

Pod has a question about roses in his homework this week. To display the record with information about the rose, he needs to type **rose** into the **Name** field. The computer searches through all the records and finds the one that Pod has asked for.

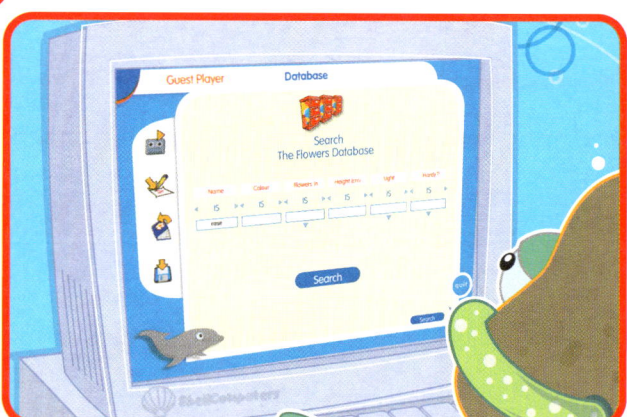

Questions

1   How would you find the record for the buttercup?

2   How would you find all the plants that like shade?

Things to do at the computer

1 Can you search for all the plants that have red flowers? Hint: type **red** in the **Colour** field. Display the result as a list. How many are there?

2 How many plants have orange flowers? Hint: type **orange** in the **Colour** field.

3 Add another new record to the database with information about the poppy.

Towards late spring, the fields of Spark Island are full of bright red poppies. Growing to 60cm in height, this hardy plant enjoys full sunlight.

4 Search for all the red flowers again. Is the poppy included in the list?

5 Search for the record about the sunflower. Hint type **sunflower** in the **Name** field. How tall can it grow?

6 Can you search for all the plants that prefer sunny conditions? Display the records as a list.

Question

The computer quickly found the answers to your questions. Do you think it would take you longer to find the answers using your paper record cards? Try it and see!

Remember

Computer databases can search for information very quickly, even if there are lots of records.

Bar charts

Pod and Piska have sorted their record cards by the colour of the flower. They then drew this **bar chart** to show the results.

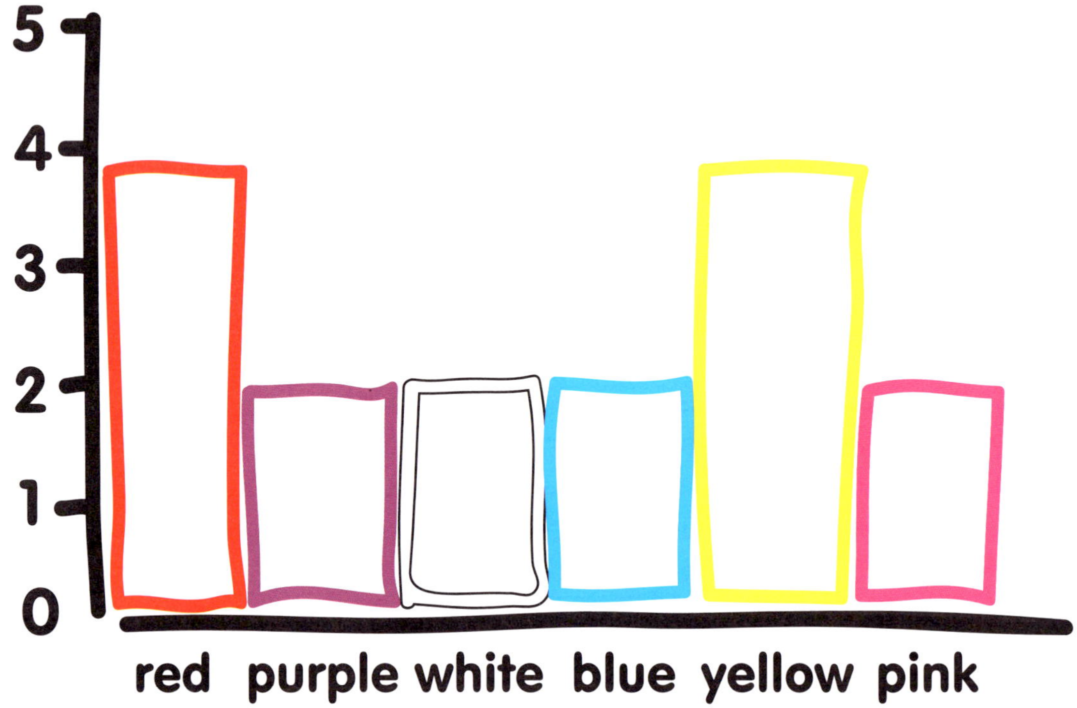

```
5
4
3
2
1
0
   red  purple white  blue  yellow  pink
```

Things to do

Can you draw a bar chart to show how many plants prefer sun, shade or like a mixture of sun and shade?

1 Sort your paper records into groups and then count the number of records in each group.

2 Draw your bar chart and colour the bars.

Questions

1 How many plants like sunny conditions?

2 How many prefer to be in the shade?

3 How many like to have some sun and some shade?

The computer database program can also draw bar charts. In today's lesson Pod and Piska will be looking at when plants flower. Meera is going to show them how many plants flower in each season of the year.

She clicks on the **Bar Chart** button and a blank chart is displayed.

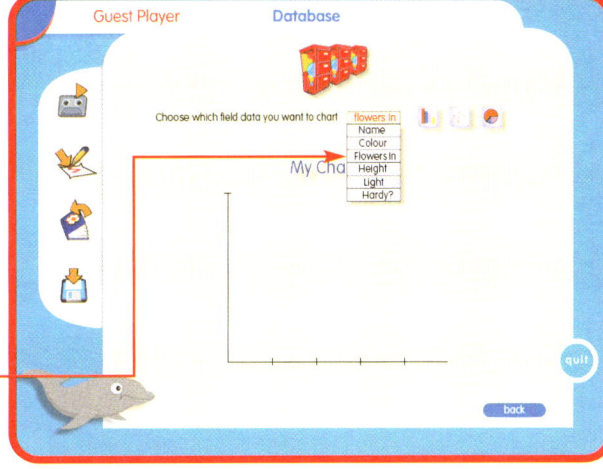

Flowers in

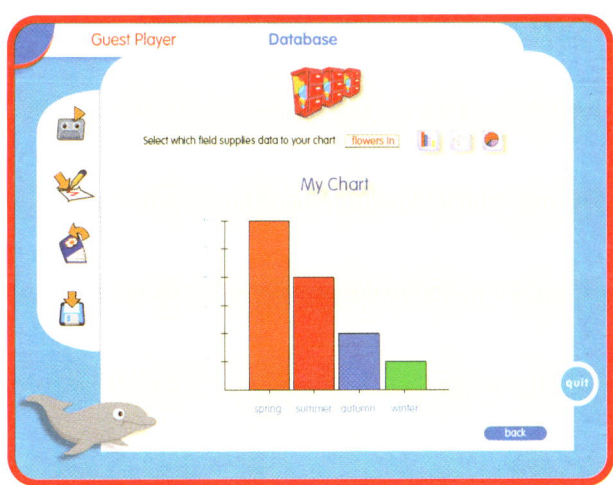

Meera picks the field from the drop down list that she wants to display on the bar chart. The bar chart is then displayed.

Questions

1 How many plants flower in winter?

2 Why do you think that most plants start to flower in spring?

Things to do at the computer

1 Use the computer to draw a bar chart to show the colours of the flowers. Hint: Select the **Colour** field. Does it look the same as the one drawn by Pod and Piska?

2 Use the computer to draw a bar chart to show how many plants prefer, sun, shade or a mixture of both. Hint: Select the **Light** field. Does it look the same as the bar chart you drew?

Remember

Bar charts can be used to display database information.

Friends database

You are going to make a database to hold information about you and your friends. Before you can add any records to your database you need to find out the answers to some questions.

Is your friend a boy or a girl? | boy/girl

What colour is your friend's hair?
blonde
light brown
dark brown
red

How long is their hair?
long
medium
short

What colour are their eyes?
blue
green
brown
hazel

Does your friend wear glasses?
Yes
No

Your database will include the fields shown on this record card. Fill in at least six paper record cards with information about your friends. Use the picture on page 40 to help you decide what information to use. You can also draw a picture of them if you want to!

Name:

Boy or Girl:

Hair colour:

Hair length:

Eye colour:

Glasses?:

To do at the computer

1 Add your records to the computer database. To save you having to do a lot of typing, you will be given choices for the fields. Just click on the answer.

2 Can you find the record for your best friend? Hint: search for their name using the **Name** field.

3 Can you find the records for everyone with long hair? Hint: click on **long** in the **Hair length** field.

4 Can you draw a bar chart to show how many people have each eye colour? Does it look like this one?

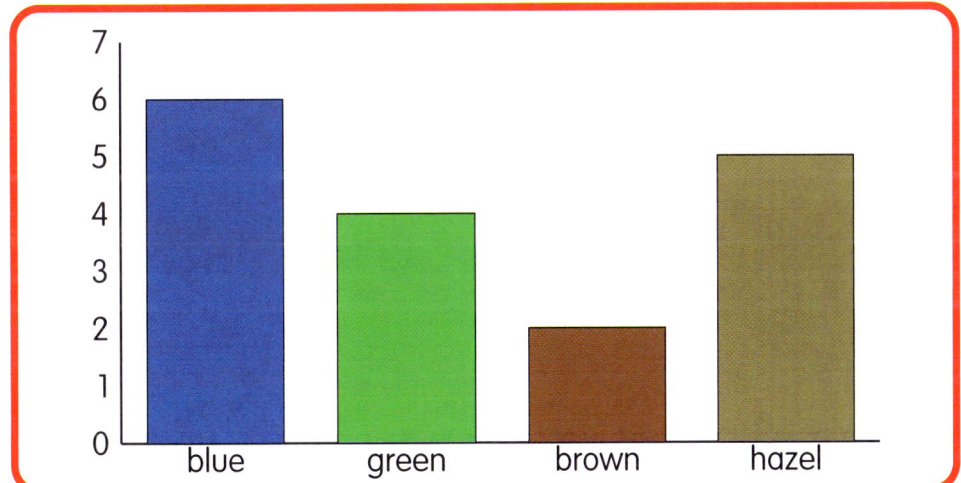

Simulate work or play

People who are learning a new skill can use computer simulations to help them. They can use the **simulation** program to practise until they are ready to do the real job.

These people use a computer simulation program to help them do their job:

This simulation program helps the architect design a new house.

This flight simulator is used to teach pilots how to fly an aeroplane.

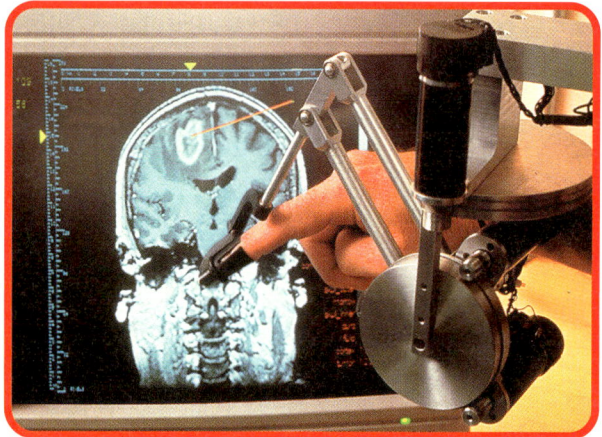

This important simulation teaches doctors how to operate on patients.

This simulation program teaches future captains how to sail a ship.

Questions

1 Why do you think that these simulation programs are used? How do they help?

2 Can you think of any other times when a simulation program can be used to help someone with their work?

Simulation programs are used to show what it was like in the past and what it might be like in the future. With a simulation, you can experience something that you are unlikely to do in real life. By watching a computer simulation you can find out what it would be like to walk on the moon!

Scientists use this simulation program when making new medicines.

This simulation shows how the land and sea have moved to make today's world.

This simulation show us what a building on Mars might look like in the future.

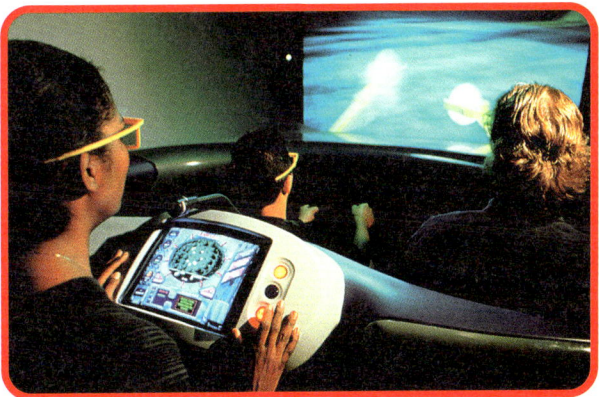

This simulation lets you experience a submarine ride without going underwater!

Questions

1 Can you think of any other computer simulations that would be useful for scientists?

2 Can you think of any other computer simulations that could be used for fun?

3 Can you think of a computer simulation that you would like to use?

Remember

Computer simulations have lots of different uses. They are used for work and play.

In control

With most simulation programs you are in control. If you are using a flight simulator you are in control of the plane, you steer the plane and press the buttons. It is down to you whether the plane lands or crashes!

Computer games are also simulations that you control. Whether you win or lose the game depends on how well you play. You are involved in the simulation and your decisions change the way it works. Some games need lots of skill and others are quite simple to play.

With other simulations you just watch, and see what happens.

Wick

Fort William

Edinburgh

Belfast

Newcastle

Manchester

Birmingham

Norwich

Cardiff

London

Plymouth

St Helier

FRIDAY 1130

With this simulation you can see what the weather is expected to do today.

Things to do at the computer

Have a look at some of these simulations for yourself.

1 Rollercoaster ride.

2 See today's weather forecast develop.

3 Make a mummy.

Questions

1 Which simulation seemed the most real? Why was this?

2 Which simulation did you enjoy the most?

3 Which simulation was the most useful? Why was this?

Remember

You need to control some computer simulations and others you just watch.

How plants grow

Each part of the plant does a different job.

The seeds make new plants.

The flowers attract insects that pollinate the plant.

The stem takes the water from the roots to all the other parts of the plant.

The leaves use the sunlight to make food.

The roots keep the plant firmly anchored in the ground. They take in water.

You can do experiments to see what happens if the different parts of the plant cannot do their job.

What happens if the plant is in a cold place?

What happens if the plant does not get enough water?

What happens if the plant does not get any sunlight?

What happens if insects do not pollinate the plant?

How plants grow

If you do not have the time to do all these experiments you can use a computer simulation program to see what happens.

Pod and Piska are using a plant simulation program because there are no land plants under the sea in Sparklantis so they cannot do the experiments themselves! A computer simulation program is just what they need.

For the first experiment they have to choose a place for their new plant. Pod chooses a warm place, but Piska chooses one that is much colder. The computer simulation shows them what will happen as their plants grow.

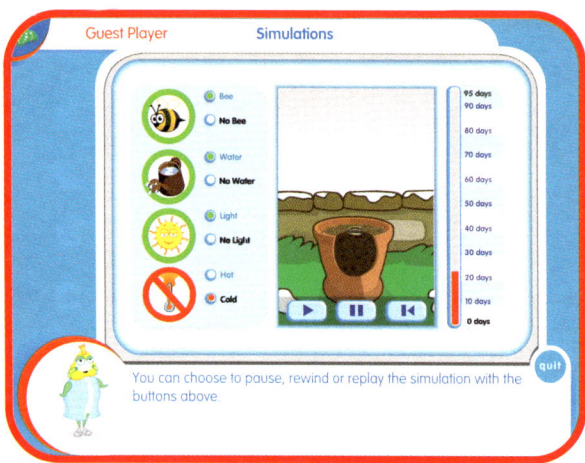
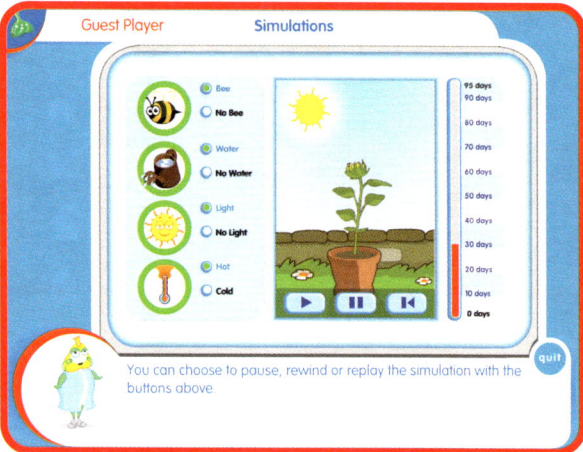

Questions

1 Which plant do you think is Pod's and which is Piska's?

2 Why is the plant in the cold place not growing?

Things to do at the computer

Have a go at using the plant simulation program.
See what happens if:

1 the plant is grown in cold weather;

2 the plant does not get enough water;

3 the plant does not get any sunlight;

4 the plant is not pollinated by insects.

Pod and Piska have used the simulation program. Meera the dolphin wants to know what they thought of it.

Did you enjoy the simulation?

Simulation programs are very useful but they do not always cover everything. Some seeds do not grow even if they have all the right conditions.

Questions

What did you think of the simulation program? Can you help Meera make it better by answering her questions?

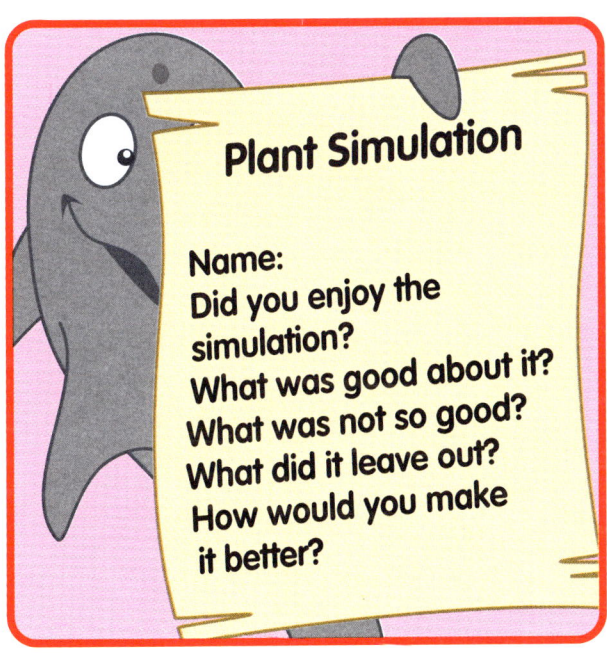

Plant Simulation

Name:
Did you enjoy the simulation?
What was good about it?
What was not so good?
What did it leave out?
How would you make it better?

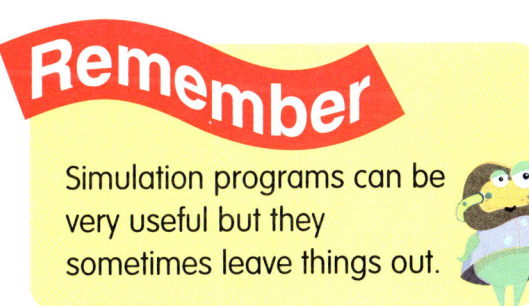

Remember

Simulation programs can be very useful but they sometimes leave things out.

Sending messages

People have found many different ways to communicate over the years.

1 American Indians used smoke signals to communicate over many miles.

2 As long ago as 1800BC, the Egyptians sent letters by boat or donkey.

3 In 1795 the British Navy used semaphore flags to send messages from London to Portsmouth.

4 Pigeons were used to send mail to and from Paris during the war with Prussia in 1870.

5 In 1860, the pony express provided the fastest mail delivery across parts of America.

6 Morse Code was introduced as a method of communicating in 1837. It was a code using a series of dots and dashes.

Thing to do

Write down at least one good and one bad thing about each of these methods of communicating over distance.

Over the years, we have found much better ways to communicate over long distances.

1 By 1897 postmen were delivering letters to every home in England.

2 In 1901, Marconi sent a radio signal across the Atlantic Ocean.

3 Alexander Graham Bell invented the telephone in 1876 and by 1884 people were making long distance calls.

4 Xerox sold its first fax machine, called a Telecopier, in 1966.

5 Over the last few years people have been communicating using **e-mail**.

6 Text messaging is the latest way to communicate with a friend.

Sending messages

We can now telephone someone wherever they live in the world, we can send e-mails at any time of the day and chat to our friends by sending text messages. It is easy to communicate.

Things to do

Imagine that you want to send the following messages. Decide which method of communication you would use. Make a note of why you would choose that method.

1 Send a Christmas card to a friend living in France.
2 Ask your friend if they are going to football practice.
3 Send your grandparents a photo of you in the school play.
4 Send thank you notes to your relatives for your birthday presents.
5 You notice a fire in a house and need to send for a fire engine.

Questions

1 Which do you think is the quickest way to send a message?
2 If you wanted to send a secret message, which method would you use?
3 If you wanted to send a very important message, which method would you use?

There are many different ways that messages can be sent over a distance. Choose the best method for the message you need to send.

E-mail penpals

Electronic mail (e-mail) is mail that is sent by computer. First, you need to type in the address of the person you want to send a message to. You then type in your message and click on the **Send** button. The message is sent directly to your friend. When they next use their computer they will be able to read your message and send you a reply.

E-mail penpals

E-mail addresses are different to usual addresses. No two addresses are exactly the same.

sally.brown@treetopsprimary.co.uk

DGreen@GreensDental.co.uk

Maggie@fineflowers.co.uk

You write an e-mail message in just the same way as you would write a letter. Pod has sent this e-mail to Sally Brown at Treetops Primary School.

From: pod@sparklearning.com
Sent: Wednesday, June 15th, 3.30 p.m.
To: sally.brown@treetopsprimary.co.uk

Hi Sally,
My name is Pod and I live in Sparklantis with my sister Piska. I go to Sparklantis Primary School which is close to where I live and my favourite subject is science. I have lots of hobbies. I love to have adventures with Piska and I am very good at telling stories. Please write and tell me all about you.

From Pod.

From: pod@sparklearning.com

Sent: Wednesday, June 15th, 3.30p.m.
To: sally.brown@treetopsprimary.co.uk

Hi Sally
My name is Pod and I live in Sparklantis with my sister Piska. I go to Sparklantis Primary School which is close to where I live and my favourite subject is science. I have lots of hobbies. I love to have adventures with Piska and I am very good at telling stories. Please write and tell me all about you.

From Pod.

Things to do at the computer

1 Write an e-mail to Pod. Tell him about yourself, your name, about your family and your hobbies.

2 Check your letter before you send it. Make sure that your spelling and punctuation are correct and that your message is clear and easy to understand.

Remember

Sending an e-mail is similar to sending a letter, but with e-mail the message is sent electronically. It is much quicker to communicate by e-mail. The message is delivered straight away; a letter can take days to arrive.

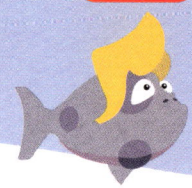

Message received

When you receive a new email you will see it in your Inbox. Pod has received an e-mail from Sally. He can see the e-mail listed in his Inbox. Sally has told him all about herself.

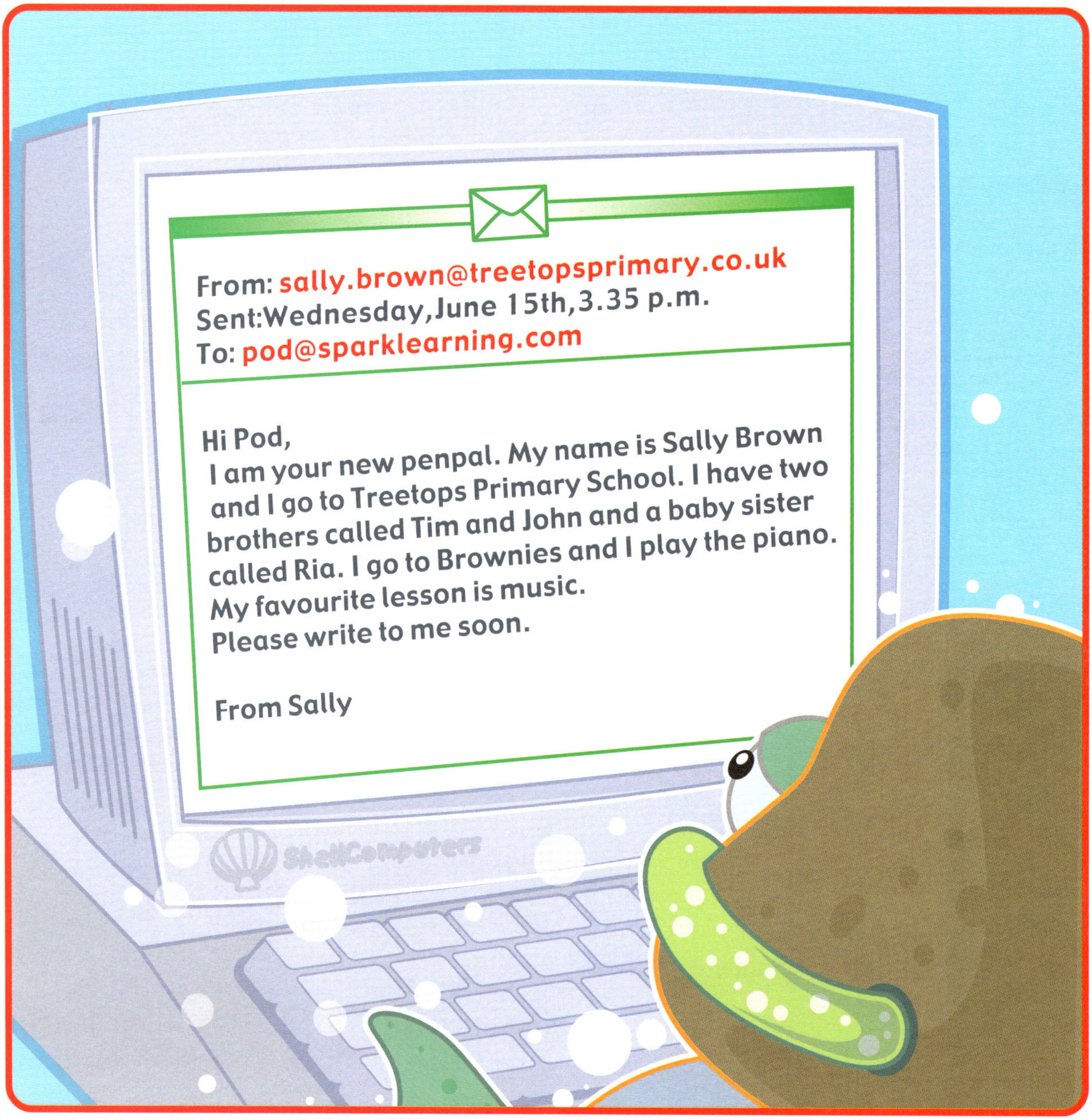
From: sally.brown@treetopsprimary.co.uk
Sent:Wednesday,June 15th,3.35 p.m.
To: pod@sparklearning.com
Hi Pod,
I am your new penpal. My name is Sally Brown and I go to Treetops Primary School. I have two brothers called Tim and John and a baby sister called Ria. I go to Brownies and I play the piano.
My favourite lesson is music.
Please write to me soon.
From Sally
ShellComputers

Pod is pleased to hear from Sally. He decides to add her details to his Friends database but to do this he needs to find out more about her. He clicks on the **Reply** button and types in lots of questions! When he has finished his reply he clicks on the **Send** button, to send it to her.

R E P L Y :
From: pod@sparklearning.com
Sent: Wednesday, June 15th, 3.35 p.m.
To: sally.brown@treetopsprimary.co.uk

Hi Sally,
Thanks for your email. I would like to add your details to my database of friends.
Could you please answer these questions?

Name:
Boy or Girl:
Hair colour:
Hair length:
Eye colour:
Glasses?:

Thanks! Pod.

Message received

Sally has received Pod's e-mail and she is answering his questions. Sally's teacher has suggested that she type her answers next to Pod's questions. This is known as sending an annotated reply to an e-mail.

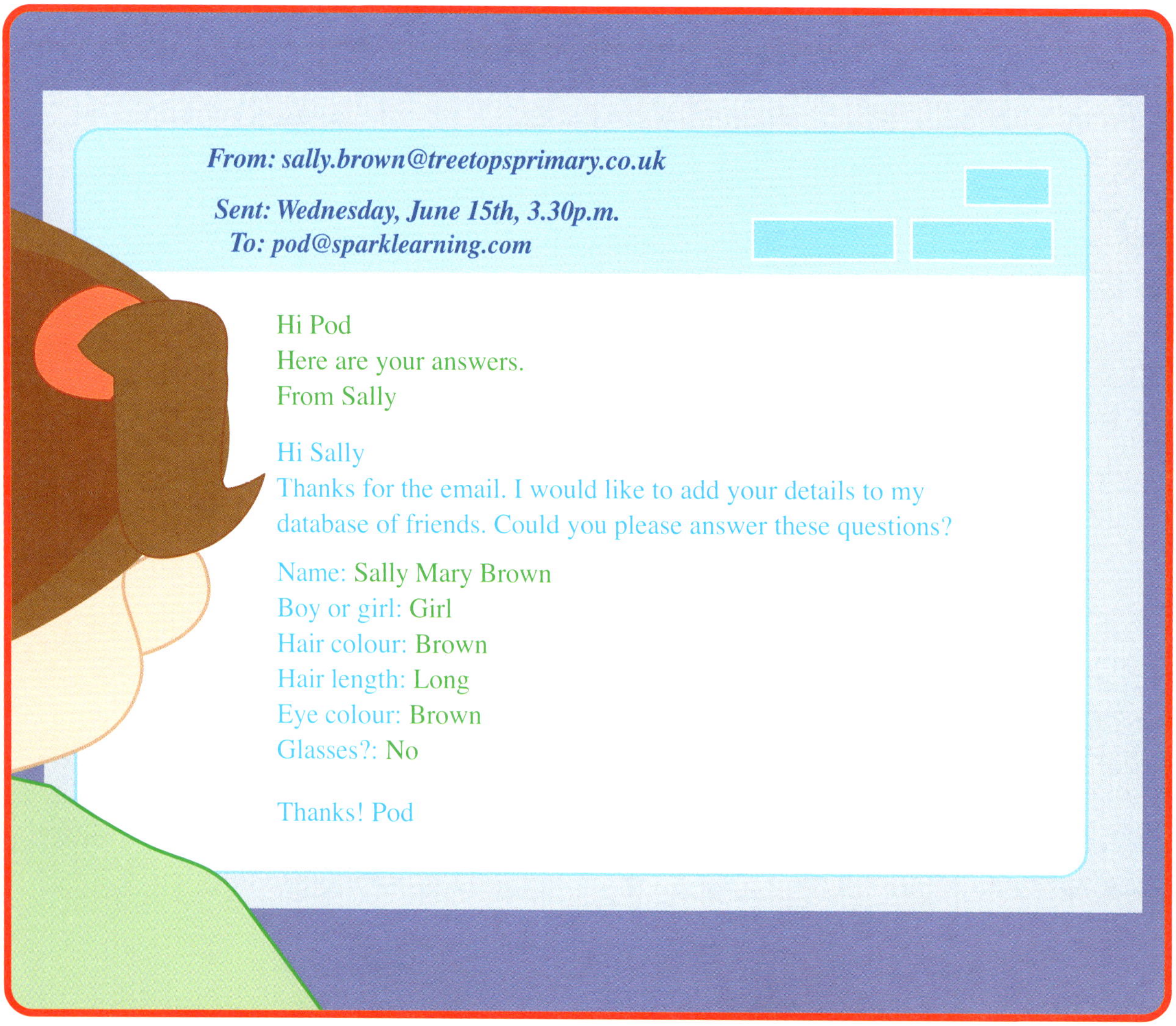

From: sally.brown@treetopsprimary.co.uk

Sent: Wednesday, June 15th, 3.30p.m.
To: pod@sparklearning.com

Hi Pod
Here are your answers.
From Sally

Hi Sally
Thanks for the email. I would like to add your details to my database of friends. Could you please answer these questions?

Name: Sally Mary Brown
Boy or girl: Girl
Hair colour: Brown
Hair length: Long
Eye colour: Brown
Glasses?: No

Thanks! Pod

Things to do at the computer

Can you add Sally's details to your database?

Remember

Sometimes it is easier to annotate a reply rather than re-typing the questions.

Attachments

Pod has received the annotated reply from Sally and has added her details to his database. He has also drawn a portrait of Sally. He is so pleased with the result he wants to send it to her! What do you think of Pod's portrait of Sally? Do you think she will like it?

It is very simple to attach a picture or other type of document to an e-mail. Most e-mail programs have a button with a picture of a paperclip. You click on that button and then find the picture or document that you want **to send as an attachment**.

Address books

If you have a lot of friends it can be handy to write their names and addresses in an **address book**. E-mail programs also have an address book. You can add the e-mail address for each of your friends to the e-mail address book. Once entered, you can select the address from the book rather than typing it in each time.

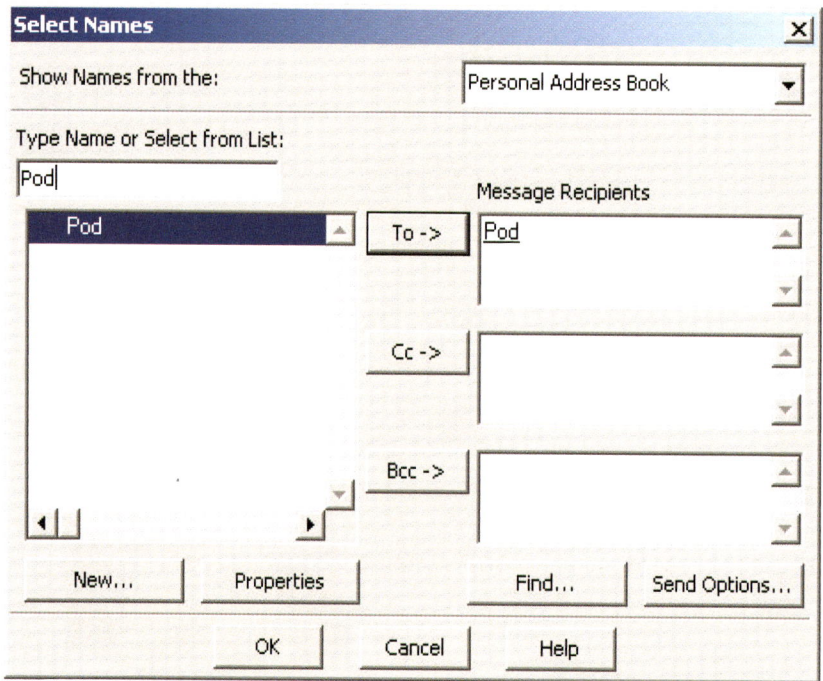

Things to do at the computer

1 Draw a picture of yourself.

2 Send Pod a new e-mail. Use your e-mail address book to select his e-mail address.

3 Write a short note and attach the picture to the e-mail before you send it.

4 Wait for a reply and see whether Pod liked your drawing!

Questions

1 Do you prefer sending a letter or an e-mail? Why is this?

2 Which is quicker?

3 Which method is best for private information?

4 Which is better if you want to keep the information?

Remember

It is easy to make a mistake when typing an e-mail address, so use the address book to select the e-mail address.

Class Project

You have spent a long time preparing information about where you live. Some of the children in your class have concentrated on the school, others on the history of your town and others on places of interest in your town.

Your class will send another school a copy of your project. In return they will send you a copy of their project. Do not forget to thank them for all their hard work!

When you receive the project, read it carefully and think about the questions that you would like to ask. Is there any information missing? If so, make a note.

When you have collected together some questions, get some of the class to e-mail the school to try and find out the answers. When you get their replies add the information or make changes to the project work.

Remember to check your e-mail Inbox. You might receive e-mails with questions about your class project.

When you have made all the changes you need, why not display the information so that the rest of the school can read it! Just think, your hard work will also be on display in another school in the country. You now know all about a town and a group of children and yet you have never even met them. It has all been down to communicating using e-mail!

CLASS PROJECT

Remember

E-mail can help you gather information and communicate with others, however far away they are.